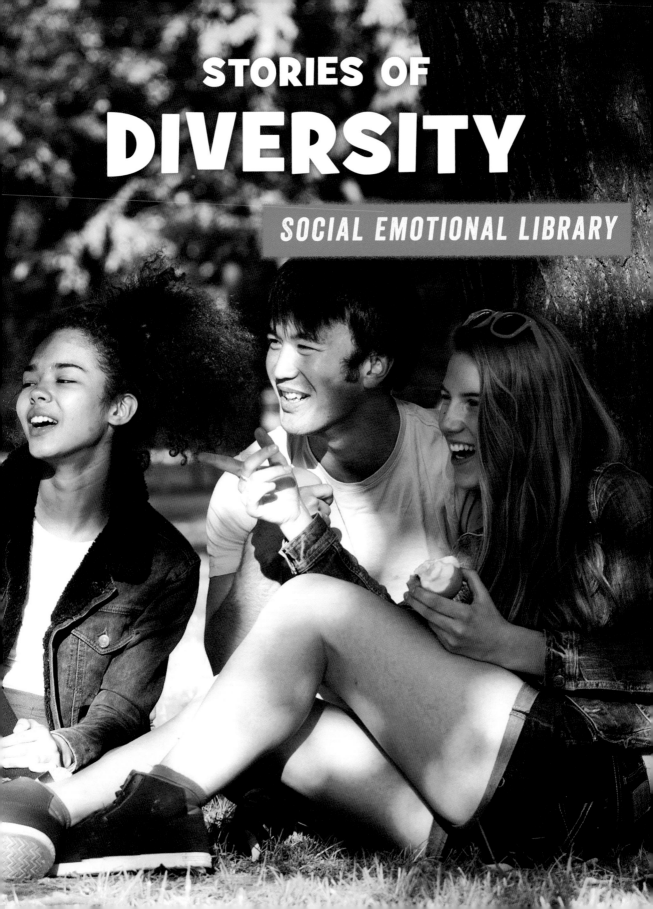

STORIES OF
DIVERSITY

Published in the United States of America by Cherry Lake Publishing
Ann Arbor, Michigan
www.cherrylakepublishing.com

Content Adviser: Satta Sarmah Hightower, www.sattasarmah.com
Reading Adviser: Marla Conn MS, Ed., Literacy specialist, Read-Ability, Inc.

Photo Credits: ©iordani/Shutterstock Images, cover, 1; ©michaeljung/Shutterstock Images, 5; ©LIFE Photo Archive/ Wikimedia, 7; ©Wikimedia, 8; ©Tim Graham / Alamy Stock Photo, 11; ©Zvonimir Atletic/Shutterstock Images, 13; ©PH1 James Franzen, USN/Wikimedia, 15; ©Popartic/Shutterstock Images, 16; ©Supermop/Shutterstock Images, 17; ©Dragon Images/Shutterstock Images, 18; ©David Harmantas/Shutterstock Images, 21; ©bogdan ionescu/Shutterstock Images, 22; ©Joe Bielawa/Flickr 25; ©carterdayne/iStock Images, 27; ©Steve Quinlan/Shutterstock Images, 28

Library of Congress Cataloging-in-Publication Data
Names: Colby, Jennifer, 1971- author.
Title: Stories of diversity / by Jennifer Colby.
Description: Ann Arbor : Cherry Lake Publishing, [2018] | Series: Social emotional library |
    Audience: Grade 4 to 6. | Includes bibliographical references and index.
Identifiers: LCCN 2017035926 | ISBN 9781534107441 (hardcover) | ISBN 9781534109421 (pdf) |
    ISBN 9781534108431 (pbk.) | ISBN 9781534120419 (hosted ebook)
Subjects: LCSH: Cultural pluralism—Juvenile literature. | Biography—Juvenile literature.
Classification: LCC HM1271 .C6344 2018 | DDC 305.092/2—dc23
LC record available at https://lccn.loc.gov/2017035926

Cherry Lake Publishing would like to acknowledge the work of The Partnership for 21st Century Learning.
Please visit www.p21.org for more information.

Printed in the United States of America
Corporate Graphics

ABOUT THE AUTHOR

Jennifer Colby is a school librarian in Michigan. She works at a school that is extremely diverse and loves learning about different cultural traditions from her students.

TABLE OF CONTENTS

CHAPTER 1

What Is Diversity?

Are you friends with people who are different than you? Maybe you have friends who are from another country or have a different religion than you. Maybe they speak a foreign language or have a different skin color than yours. If so, you respect **diversity**. Diversity requires having **tolerance** or feeling **empathy** for others who have different beliefs and backgrounds. You respect diversity when you accept others who are not like you. In our large world, there are many examples of celebrating and defending racial, social, religious, and gender diversity.

There are over 190 countries in the world.

CHAPTER 2

Mohandas Gandhi

Defending diversity can mean taking risks. As a political leader, Mohandas Gandhi suffered for the sake of diversity. During British rule, he protested for the rights of the people of India. He insisted on being nonviolent in his struggle for racial and religious equality. He became an inspiration to many people during and after his lifetime.

Born in the British-ruled Indian Empire on October 2, 1869, Gandhi was a lifelong vegetarian. He believed that as long as other food was available, animals should not be killed. Gandhi left India after high school to study law in London. But before leaving, he promised his mother that he would not adopt the vices of an English lifestyle, which included eating meat and drinking alcohol. While in England, he joined a Theosophical

Gandhi was a lawyer in Johannesburg, South Africa.

Society, a group that embraced racial diversity and whose aim was to study all religions, **philosophy**, and science.

After he became a lawyer, he returned to India. But in his first court case, he was shy and unable to question a witness. He soon left for South Africa to be the personal lawyer for a distant cousin. Like other dark-skinned people there, Gandhi faced **discrimination** and **racism**. He was beaten up when he refused to sit on the floor in a stagecoach, he was kicked to the gutter when he walked too close to a house, and he was thrown off a train after refusing to leave the first-class car.

Gandhi met with the British Secretary of State for India in 1946.

Yet, in the 21 years he was in South Africa, Gandhi developed his theory of nonviolent protest. He left South Africa to return to India in 1914 and worked in politics, seeking equal rights and voting rights for Indians under British rule. Within a few years, he became a leader of the Indian National Congress and declared independence for India. Discussions with the British went on for many years until World War II, when Gandhi demanded immediate independence. He also campaigned against any Indian association in the war. The British responded by putting

Gandhi in jail with tens of thousands of Indian political leaders. While in jail for two years, he nonviolently protested British rule through on-and-off **fasting**, interviews, and letter writing, in hopes of securing India's independence.

In 1945, a new party took power in the British government, and discussions for independence began again. But the plan that was agreed upon was one that Gandhi did not like. India was partitioned, or separated, along religious lines. It became two independent nations: a Hindu India and a Muslim Pakistan. Many people were forced to move to the nation of their religion, and more than half a million people were killed in religious protests. On January 30, 1948, Gandhi was shot to death by a Hindu man who believed that Gandhi had been too supportive of Muslims during the partition of India.

Throughout his political career, Mohandas Gandhi promoted a **diverse** society by accepting different religions, races, and **castes**. He said, "Tolerance is the only thing that will enable persons belonging to different religions to live as good neighbors and friends." His nonviolent brand of protest encouraged others to seek out justice through discussion, fasting, and political actions.

CHAPTER 3

Mother Teresa

Have you ever helped a friend or family member who was sick? Sometimes people are cast out of society because of an illness. With little access to health care and financial support, these people have no one to help them. Mother Teresa of Calcutta, India, saw the suffering of these **untouchables** and devoted her life to their care.

She was born Anjezë Gonxhe on August 26, 1910, in the Ottoman Empire (now Macedonia). Baptized in the Roman Catholic faith, she decided at a young age to commit to a religious life. In 1928, she left home to begin her religious training as a nun with the Sisters of Loreto in Ireland. Nuns are members

Mother Teresa helped sick people of different cultures overseas.

of a religious community of women, also known as a convent, who vow to live in poverty, maintain **chastity**, and be **obedient** to God. Many nuns dedicate their lives to serving others.

Sister Teresa soon moved to India to start teaching at a school. In 1937, she took her final professional vows and became "Mother" Teresa. She witnessed the poverty and unhappiness of her schoolchildren and their families over the 20 years she served at the school. She decided that she wanted to spend her life helping the poor and unwell. Mother Teresa left her convent in 1948, and she began missionary work in Calcutta, living with the people she assisted.

Now on her own, Mother Teresa established the Missionaries of Charity. The organization would care for "the hungry, the naked, the homeless, the crippled, the blind, the **lepers**, all those people who feel unwanted, unloved, uncared for throughout society, people that have become a burden to the society and are shunned by everyone." Its mission work grew to include multiple hospitals, orphanages, and leper houses throughout India. By 1997, the Missionaries of Charity had 610 foundations in 123 countries, serving the poorest of the poor.

Her work to treat the poor of India with respect brought the world's attention to the problems of the lower castes of Indian society. In 1979, Mother Teresa received the Nobel Peace Prize "for work undertaken in the struggle to overcome poverty and distress." She refused to attend the standard ceremonial banquet for Nobel award winners. Instead, she asked that the $192,000 cost of the ceremony be given to the poor in India.

Mother Teresa started many children's homes.

In 1997, Mother Teresa's health was failing, and she resigned as head of the Missionaries of Charity. She died later that year. But her legacy of helping diverse groups of people lives on. More than 1 million Missionaries of Charity workers around the world run soup kitchens, counseling programs, schools, orphanages, and hospitals for people with leprosy, HIV/AIDS, and **tuberculosis**. Her commitment to helping the less fortunate and unwanted still inspires many others to do the same.

CHAPTER 4

The O'Leary Family

Would you give up your comfortable life to help those not as fortunate as you? That is exactly what the O'Leary family of Danielson, Connecticut, did. For more than 10 years, the O'Learys **sponsored** Laotian **refugees**. The family invited them to live and work in their community. Their acts of generosity changed the lives of the Laotian people they assisted. Their compassion encouraged diversity in the lives of the residents of their small Connecticut town.

On June 24, 1979, the O'Leary family watched a television news program about the difficulties of Vietnamese boat people, and they were inspired. They wanted to help citizens of Southeast Asia who were fleeing their war-torn countries. "We were **captivated**, horrified, and heartbroken," explained their

Many Vietnamese people left their country on boats.

daughter. The next morning, they called a charity organization and signed up to adopt a refugee family.

The end of the Vietnam War left hundreds of thousands of Vietnamese, Cambodian, and Laotian citizens in desperate situations. **Despotic** leaders ruled their countries, and many lives were threatened. From 1975 to the early 1990s, 796,310 boat people and a total of 2 million refugees left their homelands by boat to seek safety and a new life in another country. Many of these refugees **resettled** in North America, Australia, and Europe, but hundreds of thousands of others died during their journeys.

The Vietnam War affected nearby Laos and Cambodia.

The O'Learys first adopted a family of nine Laotian refugees. The family's six children enrolled in the local school, and the father started working in the O'Learys's flower shop. At first, life wasn't easy for the refugee family or the O'Learys. The children couldn't speak English, and the closest interpreter lived more than an hour away. The O'Leary family received threatening phone calls and hate mail, and their flower shop lost business. But the O'Learys continued on and developed a system to help even more Laotian refugees.

The O'Learys meant to adopt one child and instead sponsored a family.

Eventually, the O'Learys's community accepted the refugee families.

By working at the flower shop, Thong Phommachanh, the father of the Laotian family, earned enough money to get an apartment for his family. After they moved, the O'Learys sponsored another refugee family. When the second family was also independently settled, they helped another family. Additionally, each refugee family that was now settled helped the next new family.

Soon the town had more than 500 Laotian refugees who became involved in their new community. The O'Leary's daughter later said, "Our quiet little town became more cultured, and residents eventually learned more about their new neighbors and began to embrace them." The school system developed programs for the refugee children, and local businesses appreciated the hardworking attitude of the Laotian adults.

By picking up a refugee family at a Boston airport in 1979, the O'Leary family promoted diversity in their small town. Now Danielson and nearby Killingly, Connecticut, are homes to Laotian communities. The towns are among the nation's 50 cities with the highest number of Laotian citizens. The O'Leary family's compassion for those who are different inspired acceptance in their community.

Do You Support Diversity?

Are you accepting of others? Do you think that all people are equal no matter where they come from or what they believe? If so, then you support diversity. A respectful person tries to understand others. This person is a good example for others to look up to and follow. Think about diverse people in your life who inspire and encourage others to accept diversity.

CHAPTER 5

Not in Our Town

What do you do when you see someone being mean to another person? Do you stand up and try to stop it? In 1993, a small group of residents in Billings, Montana, stood up to religious **intolerance** that was **infiltrating** their town. Their actions began a worldwide movement of acceptance and diversity called Not in Our Town.

Not in Our Town's aim at the local level is "to stop hate, address bullying, and build safe, inclusive communities for all." Communities all around the world have adopted the movement to end incidents of hate and to create safe environments for their citizens. The Not in Our Town movement has grown to include projects called Not in Our School and Not on Our Campus.

Not In Our Town was launched after Billings was shown in a PBS film.

Both encourage developing a community of "upstanders," or people who don't ignore hate incidents but instead support victims of intolerance.

But before there were upstanders or a movement, there was a big problem in Billings. For years, the community's 80,000 mostly white and mostly Christian residents had put up with racist groups that were intolerant of diversity. Gradually, these groups' beliefs led to outward expressions of hate toward anyone who was not a white Christian.

The menorah's seven lamps have different meanings for Jewish people.

The racist groups committed acts of hatred against the **minority Jewish** population. They handed out flyers, smashed windows, and destroyed Jewish cemeteries. In response, a multifaith group started asking their congregations to draw thousands of menorahs to display all over town. The menorah is a religious symbol of a Jewish holiday. The racist groups would destroy the menorahs, but when they did, hundreds more replaced them. Homes and businesses all over town displayed menorahs, encouraging diversity and acceptance of the smaller Jewish community. Uniting all faiths in this effort helped to reduce the hate crimes against the Jewish people.

Soon after, a filmmaker produced *Not in Our Town*, a half-hour film about the community's response to hate. This title became the name of the movement for those seeking to stand up to **intimidation**, **bigotry**, and racism. Today, there are thousands of communities, schools, and college campuses that embrace the Not in Our Town philosophy. Their work to protect people of all races and religions represents the true spirit of diversity.

Diversity in the Workplace

What if everyone at work came from the same background and had the same perspective? Diversity is important for having a successful career because if everyone was similar, nothing would change for the better. It is helpful to surround yourself with different individuals so that you can share ideas and become more understanding of others. In fact, diverse peers can draw from their experiences to point out things like unfairness due to skin color, language, or heritage that you may not have noticed happening!

CHAPTER 6

Cities Showing Acceptance of Gay Pride

Do you have friends or family members who are **gay**, **lesbian**, or **transgender**? It is important to support them in any way you can. Many people around the world who identify as lesbian, gay, **bisexual**, transgender, or questioning (LGBTQ) face discrimination. To confront this, many cities prominently show their appreciation for the diverse LGBTQ community through events and displays.

Minneapolis lit the whole Interstate 35 bridge with rainbow lights.

The city of Seattle, Washington, shows its support every year by hosting the Pride festival, parade, and related events over the course of a month. In 2017, the festival celebrated its 43rd annual parade. Businesses—including banks, airlines, retail stores, hospitals, computer makers, and coffee companies—participated in the 2 1/2-hour parade alongside teachers and church congregations. All of the Pride events encourage Seattle's citizens to be accepting of others.

In 2017, the Dublin Front Runners A.C. in Ireland organized the Sixth Annual 5K Pride Run. The city's running club is open to the LGBTQ community and friends. It was organized in 2005 and now has 180 members, making it Ireland's largest LGBTQ sports group. The run is one of the first events in Dublin's weeklong pride festival, which includes a parade, workshops, dances, and a soccer match. It is a celebration of diversity in modern Ireland.

The Gay Games began in 1980 and are held every four years in different cities. The games encourage inclusivity for LGBTQ athletes, who have historically been left out of the athletic community. The Ninth International Gay Games were held in August 2014, in Cleveland, Ohio. They included diversity training for local businesses to promote acceptance of LGBTQ people in the workplace. The 2018 Gay Games will be held in Paris, France.

In addition to holding large events, Minnesota embraces the LGBTQ community with a colorful display of support. In 2013, it became the 12th state to legalize gay marriage. That same year, the city of Minneapolis celebrated the milestone by lighting the entire 2,000-foot (610 meters) Interstate 35 bridge that crosses the Mississippi River with rainbow-colored lights. This was an

The rainbow flag is a symbol of lesbian, gay, bisexual, and transgender pride.

Pride events try to be inclusive of different identities.

especially **poignant** celebration because the same bridge had collapsed in 2007, killing 13 people and injuring more than 100.

From elaborate displays to large events, communities around the world have shown a commitment to the acceptance of LGBTQ culture. Communities that model diversity encourage others to do the same, promoting freedom of expression and safety for all.

What Have You Learned About Diversity?

The world is made up of people of different races, religions, and beliefs, but sometimes with diversity comes intolerance. Throughout the years, many groups have been discriminated against because of hatred toward a person's race, religion, gender, or partner preference. Many times, displays of support for diversity have triumphed over these acts of hate. People in a diverse country learn from one another, which encourages acceptance of others around the world. In a global economy and society, understanding and accepting differences promotes kindness and peace.

Think About It

How Can You Support Diversity?

You can be more tolerant if you accept others and their differences. This may be hard to do if you live in a community of people who are more alike than not. Learn about different cultures by asking your parents or teachers to help you reach out to others—you can communicate through letters, blogs, and video conferencing.

For More Information

Further Reading

Abramovitz, Melissa. *Hate Crimes in America*. Minneapolis: Essential Library, 2017.

Helfand, Lewis. *Mother Teresa: Angel of the Slums*. New Delhi: Campfire, 2013.

Quinn, Jason. *Gandhi: My Life Is My Message*. New Delhi: Campfire, 2014.

Websites

ACLU—LGBT Youth
https://www.aclu.org/issues/lgbt-rights/lgbt-youth
This website has resources to help understand and support LGBT youth.

Not In Our Town—About Us
https://www.niot.org/about-us
This is the official website for the Not In Our Town movement.

Vietnamese Boat People Museum Project—Project Summary
www.vietboatpeoplemuseum.ca/en/project-summary/
Learn about the proposed Vietnamese Boat People Museum in Ottawa, Canada.

GLOSSARY

bigotry (BIG-uh-tree) hatred for people who are a different race, religion, or nationality than yours

bisexual (bye-SEKS-yoo-uhl) a person who is attracted to both men and women

captivated (KAP-tih-vay-tid) had your attention held by something

castes (KASTS) a division of society based on differences of wealth, rank, or occupation

chastity (CHAS-tih-tee) the state of not having sex with anyone

despotic (deh-SPOT-ik) describing a ruler who has total power and who often uses that power in cruel and unfair ways

discrimination (dis-krim-ih-NAY-shun) unfair treatment of different people, especially because of race, age, sex, sexual preference, and economic status

diverse (dih-VURS) made up of people who are different from each other

diversity (dih-VURS-ih-tee) a variety of different things or people

empathy (EM-puh-thee) the feeling that you understand another person's experiences and emotions

fasting (FAST-ing) not eating food for a period of time

gay (GAY) a man who is attracted to other men

infiltrating (IN-fil-trayt-ing) slowly becoming more common (in a bad way)

intimidation (in-tim-ih-DAY-shuhn) the act of making someone afraid

intolerance (in-TAH-lur-uhns) the act of not willing to allow or accept something

Jewish (JOO-ish) someone who follows the religion of Judaism, a faith that believes in God

lepers (LEP-urz) people who have leprosy, which is a serious disease that causes painful rough areas on the skin and badly damages nerves and flesh

lesbian (lez-BEE-en) a woman who is attracted to other women

minority (mye-NOR-ih-tee) a group of people of a particular race, nationality, or religion living among a larger group of a different race, nationality, or religion

obedient (oh-BEE-dee-uhnt) willing to do what someone tells you to do

philosophy (fuh-LAH-suh-fee) ideas about how to live

poignant (POIN-yuhnt) causing strong feelings

racism (RAY-siz-uhm) poor treatment of, or violence against, people because of their race or the color of their skin

refugees (REF-yoo-jeez) people who have been forced to leave a country because of war or for religious or political reasons

resettled (ree-SET-uhld) to live in a new area after leaving an old one

sponsored (SPON-serd) gave money and support to a person or program

tolerance (TAH-lur-uhns) the willingness to respect or accept the customs, beliefs, or opinions of others

transgender (tranz-JEN-dur) a person who does not identify with the gender of their birth

tuberculosis (tuh-bur-kyuh-LOH-sis) a serious disease that mainly affects the lungs

untouchables (uhn-TUHCH-uh-buhlz) people who are ignored by others and thought to be unimportant

INDEX